I0482178

33

Things You Can Do

Today

To Skyrocket
Your
KINDLE SALES

**Learn the secrets the pros use to drive
sales to incredible levels!**

No part of this book may be redistributed altered or
links removed.

© 2001 2ndEmpireMedia llc.
For more rare and hard to find books see us at

www.2ndEmpireMedia.Com

General Santos City, Philippines

Check out more recent titles from us

Power Profits!

Power Profits! Cash Flow Revolution

63 Ways to DRIVE MORE TRAFFIC to your website

How to WRITE 30 BOOKS in 30 DAYS

101 TOTALLY FREE ways to market your website or blog

How To Build a YouTube Money Machine

The 10 Principles of ENDLESS WEALTH

About the author

Danial Barron Howe is the author of over 350 books (under
multiple pen names) ranging from business and online
income to health and wellness. He is the founder of six
multinational businesses including **2ndEmpireMedia**, the
publisher of this book and TheMinuteMarketer.Com , a
rapidly growing community catering to the ongoing
education of information marketers.

Dan has been involved in the information marketing
business ever since he wrote his first book, ***POWER
PROFITS!*** Nearly a decade and a half ago. Since that time
he has gone on to sell over 750,000 books in both printed
and electronic form as well as numerous audio, video and
other hybrid forms of informational products.

In addition to his role as an informational product producer,
he holds several degrees including a Masters in mechanical
engineering and design as well as degrees in psychology
and biomechanics. He is a lifelong tinkerer artist and
visionary innovator with a passion for improving
efficiencies of systems such as those found within this
book.

Forward

Can you really expect amazing results from do it yourself-promotion?
Believe it or not, the answer is "*yes*"! I have wrote over 350 books in my career. I have never turned to anyone else to help me in my promotional efforts. I don't use virtual assistants (Even though I live in the Philippines and have access to innumerable sources for them.) and I don't buy traffic from places like Fiverr (that most often turn out to be scams anyway!).

For me, promotion is a *personal thing* I created these works myself and nobody knows them better than I do. Call me a "control freak", but I like to have my hands on all facets of the business, from production all the way through to promotion and delivery. Because of this, I have sold over 11,250,000 books in both printed and electronic form over the last 15+ years.

I can't write your books for you, nor can I market them for you. What I *will do for you* is teach you how to use the simplest, most effective ideas that will bring you results incredibly quick. My methods work! And they will set you apart from those that never seem to *strike gold* with Amazon, despite otherwise having very marketable ideas.

What you can expect from this book.
I love to teach. Despite what many people would consider "*a dyslexic disadvantage*", I love to write too! I once heard it said that "*you don't really know what you know until you have to teach it to someone else!*" I'm often surprised by the number of amazing ideas that pour out of me when I'm

in the zone and able to sit down, focus and put together my latest book or course.

This book is filled with the latest, most up-to-date Kindle e-book marketing techniques available anywhere. The methods I will teach you here in this book will unlock a treasure trove of ideas and inspire a flurry of marketing activity! By the time you finish reading this book *you will have a workable series of easily implemented ideas for creating* a real income with Amazon if you choose to do so.

I am a full-time information marketer and author.
Let me be clear upfront; I refuse to fill your head full of theoretical nonsense or recycled gibberish that I've pulled from various places all over the Internet. *I am a full time professional information marketer and 350+ title book author*. I'm in the trenches each day earning a living by the skills that I've acquired over a decade and a half of actual use. I have to, this is how I feed myself and my family! If you are looking for straightforward, candid advice on what works then follow me, I will get you where you want to go!

… And now for a shameless marketing plug:
Although the information in this book will take you a long way in the understanding of promoting your kindle publishing empire, the tips found here are only a few of the many tools available to you and you should always be on the lookout for more. You wouldn't expect to build a house using just one hammer would you?

When you're ready to take your book marketing to the next level, visit me at my site. I've put together a *virtual toolbox* of resources for you to use in your promotional efforts.

www.TheMinuteMarketer.Com

Index

Preface

What does it takes to make a living as an author?
When you look at the statistics for failed business startups in general, the prospects are pretty dismal.
Why do so many fail? Generally the answer falls into three categories:

1. They are inadequately funded
2. The owners lack some essential skill or knowledge component (or at the very least a workable plan)
3. But the biggest ones are often *loss of motivation or focus…* These are quite common for most *would-be* authors.

The good news is that by using the simple techniques I'll show you in this book, all of these common stumbling blocks will be easily avoided. In addition, I will show you the best of everything I know about how to put yourself in front of as many people as possible in the most efficient way imaginable.

British Prime Minister Winston Churchill, famously addressed a graduating class. When asked to speak he stood up, walked to the podium, quietly surveyed the crowd in attendance and instead of delivering an expectedly long winded speech, he simply announced *"Never give up! Never give up!* ***Never <u>ever</u> give up!"*** and with that he returned to his seat…. *nuff said.*

Building a sustainable business with eBooks is a numbers game.
It may come across as obvious to many of you, but understanding this fact is the key to success. The misunderstanding many beginning authors have is to expect to create *a single title* that will produce a flood of traffic and income year after year. Yes, it could happen but it's not very common. So generally speaking, that type of thinking won't get you very far.

To be a successful book seller you must have as *many hooks (books) in the water* as possible at any given time. Amazon allows you to post an unlimited amount of *unique publications* and you would be hard-pressed to find many successful kindle authors that didn't take advantage of this fact. When it comes to e-books, *volume rules!* Some will make you a little bit of money, while others could make you a lot!

There is a clear case to be made for producing multiple books
The reality is that if you only put up a couple of books on Amazon (or any other eBook seller for that matter) and expect the world to beat a path to your door you're likely going to come away sorely disappointed. Amazon's kindle program is growing by leaps and bounds and its user base is currently in the multiple millions. However, there's only so much room on the top page to be a featured seller. If you're not coming up in the searches it's unlikely anyone will ever know you even exist. This presents a problem; *how will the buyers find you?* The answer rests solely on the actions that you take to actively promote your books on your own.

By creating multiple titles you can *cross-link* them together, thereby increasing the likelihood that your entire catalog of offerings will be exposed to all new readers who come across one or more of your books, even if it's only by random chance.

I'll cover more about cross-linking your titles together later on in the book, but for now I want you to understand that when it comes to producing those multiple titles, the ones who are claiming the largest amount of *Amazons search engine real estate* are the ones who come away as the biggest winners.

Relax, everything you need to succeed is already at hand.
Promotion of any kind isn't rocket science. We'll go over some of the finer points of promotion as well. My philosophy defines promotion and has finding relevant groups of interested people and letting them know where to find you (or maybe only just making a simple introduction.). I'll show you how to do all that in upcoming chapters

Let me assure you that you don't need a sparkling personality or outstanding speaking skills to promote your book either. (Even when it comes time to make a promotional Youtube video) Heck, you don't honestly need the looks of a Hollywood actor and you really don't even need a great education. I've seen several successful examples of this theory all over Amazon! All you truly need to do is a little one time work to develop a well laid out, organized presentation and some *good 'ol fashioned know how* to deliver it in the most effective manner.

What do you need MOST to be successful?

Volume! As I said before, success with Amazon is a numbers game. The more you put yourself out there, the closer you come to greater and greater success as an author and seller. Don't worry, you WILL get there, but I won't try to kid you and tell you that it doesn't take an investment of your time and effort up front to start things moving. But, just picture yourself sitting on a tropical beach while the rest of the world deposits automatic money into your account from book sales you made on Amazon. People do a lot more difficult things all over this Earth every day for the sake of a "job".

*(No doubt you've heard this "dream scenario" many times before but I can tell you **this is my reality**! Kindle publishing has allowed me to move from America to an island paradise here in the Philippines. As I sit here dictating this book I'm on the back deck of my house overlooking the crashing waves of the China Sea. Rough life eh?)*

What if I do something wrong or nobody buys my books?

Don't worry, you'll screw up sooner or later and you'll probably get involved in several unproductive activities more than once that will make you will want to give up and lick your wounds. It's happened to the best of us.

Here's my best advice; *Get over yourself!* This whole thing is a learning process and nobody learns by getting it right all the time. If you picked the wrong topic (unlikely), designed a horrible book cover (happens quite often), or just lacked the general confidence it takes to make a well presented promotional audio or video, learn from it! Make the appropriate adjustments and then move on. Never give up!

My secret:

Do you want to know a secret that I realized long ago when faced with a situation like this? We live in the digital age. NOTHING ONLINE IS PERMANENT. Amazon doesn't put a limit on the amount of corrections you can make once you've published your work. Corrections can be made at any time with just a few keystrokes and the click of a mouse. If you don't like the way something looks after glancing at it a second or third time, fix it! New potential visitors will never know how bad things used to be.

Seriously, every time you put together a new book you are beginning with a clean slate (especially if you publish your works under multiple pen names). Once you have learned the ropes, then you'll have your own workflow template to build on. The truth is there is no reason to be embarrassed or worry about ruining your reputation. Unless you are a well-known celebrity most visitors checking out your book could care less who you are, as long as what you're providing is of sufficient value to them.

The biggest mistake you can make.
The reality is; not every book on Amazon is worth a damn. No matter how amazing you may believe your offer is, or how enticing the promotional materials or book cover appear to be. It doesn't even matter how slick your description is. Bottom line: Amazon buyers vote with their wallets. If you're not making the kind of sales you had hoped for then the problem is something you're doing is not resonating with buyers, and if you fail to address this fact you will never hit the big time.

Often times beginning authors with no formal promotional training jump headlong into book ideas that they *think* the public would be interested in, without ever doing even the least little bit of research to find out if there *actually even is* a market for what they are writing!

My advice here is simple: proceed intelligently. If you're unsure of the market size for your book, test things out with a smaller, lower-priced $.99 trial (you really have nothing to lose - it's always free to write and post your books) and see what kind of traffic comes of it before getting crazy and going all out with a larger size book.

The greatest business of the 21st century.
Throughout the course of my life I have been involved in many, many different enterprises. I have been a real estate investor, television producer, professional motorcycle manufacturer, and a whole host of other things. Each business came with its benefits and drawbacks. However, few have ever provided me with the freedom to actually enjoy my life the way kindle publishing has.

I can say without a doubt that developing informational products and eBooks, then marketing them through my various sales channels such as my websites, blogs, Youtube videos and yes, even Amazon as well has been an ongoing challenge and a thrill for me.

Sure, there was a learning curve with all of it, there always is. But, once I crossed that threshold into knowledge and proficiency I was able to enjoy a lifestyle that few will ever able to experience.

If you desire a life filled with more free time, the ability to apply your creativity in myriads of ways and a potentially far better rate of pay then you're currently earning, remember the words of Winston Churchill; *"Never give up! Never give up! Never, ever give up!"*

Ready? Then let's get started!

1. Never underestimate the power of free

The controversy surrounding Amazon's free book promotion rages on amongst Kindle publishers. Some say it's a good thing while others say it's teaching the consumer to sit back and wait for prices to come down.

While there is some validity to both sides of this issue things are not always as simple as black and white and like it or not, the practice won't be discontinuing any time soon. Better to go with the flow and learn how to use it to your advantage rather than be overtaken by it while you sit and bemoan the way things used to be.

After a recent experiment, I can now say I have an entirely different view of the situation.

Is "free" really costing you anything?
It's doubtful. A great majority of the time free downloads (90% or more) are generated by users simply *loading up* their Kindle with title after title solely based on nothing other than its giveaway price. It's unlikely that person will ever even get around to reading even a portion of what he has taken for free.

The notion that a *lost sale* has occurred doesn't hold water when you consider this type of "buyer". They would prefer to spend hours and hours poring through page after page of listings on Amazon looking for the freebies, never once even considering actually paying for anything. No loss there!

What about the other 10%?
That's where we will focus our attention. When we produce a book and send it out into the Amazon system using their free book promotion program, we have an excellent opportunity to be discovered by legitimate buyers amongst the paid product. Knowing this, we can even construct a book created *solely for the purpose* of giving away that will promote our paid book agenda!

Currently Amazon requires all Kindle books to be over at least 2500 words. That's not much. Definitely more lengthy than a sales letter, but not at all what you would consider a "typical book." This left me wondering "who would buy a book with only 2500 words anyway?" The answer is not many people - *but that story changes when it's free!*

Always one to play within the rules, I tested out an idea by creating several *mini review books.* I would outline a paragraph or two about several of my books complete with links to the sale pages of each full-length book I have for sale on Amazon. Total book length 4200 words - *not too shabby!*

Next step: publish it and launch it out to the Amazon community *free of charge* for the full five allowable promotional days (You get to do this every 90 days).

Understanding the amazing power of this little concept
If you think about it, amazon allows you to promote (give away for free) your books every 3 months (4 times per year). Knowing this, you could create four unique books dedicated to this concept and can keep one in active rotation every month!*

The results are in

I tracked the results over the five days of the book's giveaway promotion and saw a 10.3% rise in average sales. That tracks pretty closely with my *10% serious buyer theory* wouldn't you say? By the way, that's 644 additional paid sales in only 5 days for those of you who are keeping score.

*Admittedly, this is a technique that could get out of control really quick if everyone started doing it and would result in Amazon banning the practice outright. Rather than risk getting too crazy, I restricted myself to only one publication just to test results.

2. Write more books

I realize this statement may seem *glaringly obvious* to some people, but the truth of it eludes a great many others. Over the years I have met no shortage of first-time authors who have their entire hopes and dreams for success pinned on one single title. Yet, as I said before, you'd be hard-pressed to find many "successful" authors who don't have a multitude of works to their credit. There is power in numbers.

In the beginning of this book I briefly discussed how successful authors understand the intelligence of having multiple titles. I personally have over 350 and I'm constantly adding more.

I know the idea of creating multiple titles (let alone hundreds of them) might seem like a Herculean task to a lot of people, but it's not as difficult as you think. I recently completed a marathon session of **30 books in 30 days** and documented my methodology for all my readers.
If you'd like to learn more about my techniques you can check it out here.

3. Build a supporting mini site

When I wrote my first book 15 years ago I knew nothing about website creation, let alone writing a book. It was all new to me back then. I had myself convinced that I needed to have a fancy website complete with all the bells and whistles in order to sell my book. Nothing could have been further from the truth!

If you currently have a website to support your book, great! If you don't then all you need is a basic website host that provides you with a free WordPress installation module. Most of the big ones do. With WordPress you can set up a simple one or two page mini website in minutes giving your fans a place to find you and read up on all your latest news.

As things begin to take off you will want to add more and more components to your website but early on in the game don't let anyone sell you on the idea that you need anything more than a good description of your book, some information about you as well as a possible way to contact you and a way to order your book directly if your visitors choose to do so.
That's it. Nothing more.

Need an example? Check this out:
www.FlipLikeThePros.Com

4. Use your website to build a fan base

As mentioned above, once sales start to pick up, it will then be time to start adding some components to your website to capitalize on the growing traffic. Again, if you're using WordPress to develop your site you have the built-in ability to add things like

- social media buttons
- blogs
- calendars
- pictures
- videos
- RSS feeds
- and most importantly of all, mailing lists

with just a few clicks of a button.

As visitors begin to frequent your website you should have these necessary components in place to harvest every visitors email so that you can let them know when your book goes on sale, has a new addition, revision or update and especially when your next book comes out!

5. Develop a "loss leader"

This idea comes from a technique used by retail stores and it's one of my favorites. Big-box stores in many major supermarket chains often times feature low cost products to draw customers in with the hope that they will buy additional items once they are in the store. Oftentimes these items are sold at breakeven (or less) prices hence the name *loss leader.*

Luckily for us we're selling an *electronic product* so there really is no "loss" *per se.* This technique differs slightly from tip #1 in that we are offering the *actual product* for sale this time and not merely a review guide describing it. The objective is still the same however; get your buyers to purchase a second, third, fourth or fifth book as a result of being drawn in from the first.

There are many different types of loss leaders you can develop, but I'm going to focus on what I term a *serialized* loss leader, meaning; *a series of books where the first chapter or whole book in a multi book series is given away for free.*

Serialized loss leaders can be distributed in several different ways:

- You could give it away for free in the traditional way during Amazon's five-day giveaway promotional period. And do this once every 90 days.

- You could attach it to the back part of a different book as a "bonus".

- You could even go off Amazon entirely and give it away on your website - smart marketers would expect visitors to enter their email or go through some sort of enrollment process to capture reader's addresses for follow up marketing before they get access however.

- You could dole it out day by day as a teaser to the your social media followers ending in a cliffhanger that results in your buyers going to Amazon to purchase the next book in the series.

The possibilities really are endless!

6. Over Deliver

If you have spent any time at all on Amazon you are well aware of Amazon's five-star rating system. Authors who produce subpar work pay a heavy price in the form of bad ratings from underwhelmed buyers and reduced sales soon follow. Faced with this knowledge it's to your advantage to always put out the highest caliber of work possible.

As your catalog of titles continues to grow you may want to give consideration to combining two titles together for the price of one or offering bonus audio for video materials, perhaps even software if the situation warrants it as part of your books basic purchase price. The idea here is to get your buyer thinking to himself *"wow, I didn't expect to get all this!"*

By over delivering to your buyer, especially early on when you don't have many reviews, you're guaranteed a much higher likelihood of four and five star feedbacks which in turn will fuel even more future sales at a quicker pace.

7. Don't Use .99 Promos

What is it about .99 items that people just love so much? There are stores all over America dedicated to this price point! Many kindles gurus tout the *"advantages"* of selling a $.99 eBook.

Bull…

Amazon currently has two pricing structures. 35% and 70%. If you are selling a book for $.99 you're getting a whopping $0.30 (actually less) for your efforts. And I'm sorry Mr. Rockefeller, you will *not* be eating steak at the Plaza Hotel tonight with that kind of payout!

All kidding aside, it doesn't make any financial sense to offer a product for less than $2.99 (that's the bare minimum it takes to move yourself into Amazons 70% commission bracket).

We've already explored *the power of using free* to further our promotional goals, and I've already demonstrated how much more traffic can be generated when there is *no barrier to entry*, so why complicate things for mere $.30? When you consider it takes over five book sales at $0.99 to match the commission of a single book sold at $2.99, it's just not worth the hassle and the time you would have to invest.

8. Sell Value-Packs

If you have 3 or more titles on a related subject, why not combine them all together and sell them as a higher priced collection (call it a value pack)?

Instead of selling one book for $2.99 you could combine three or four together and sell them for $9.99. This represents no additional effort on your part for you to produce another product for sale because you've already wrote the books long ago.

The big benefit however is you're able to repurpose your existing library to produce an additional revenue stream essentially from thin air!

9. Serialize Your Work

Readers have a short attention span these days. When you stop to consider this, it makes very little sense to offer a single book containing 300 or more pages when statistics tell us that the average reader never finishes more than 10% of every book they purchase! Think about your own collection of books for a second and I'm sure you'll see this is true.

Why not take some of your larger books and break them down into three or four shorter books each, then offer the first one of each *book series* at a lower price? This will draw your reader in and potentially gain you four sales of higher combined price instead of just one of lesser profit!

10. Sell on eBay

EBay has helped me move thousands of books over the years. While this is not a direct benefit to your Kindle sales numbers, your book can be reconfigured for distribution in other lots of places such as createspace.com obooko & more.

You should be aware however that recently eBay has changed its rules concerning eBooks sales. It's not as easy to do as it used to be. While it's not completely impossible to still sell your books on eBay, you do have to keep up-to-date on current rule changes.

The best way to sell an ebook on Ebay these days is to sell it on cd, either burned one by one on a blank disc at home or by using any one of the thousands of on demand fulfilment services to be found around the web such as trepstar.com or cdbaby.com

11. Sell on Fiverr

Another outstanding source I have been having recent success with for outside sales is Fiverr.

Fiverr is traditionally a micro job site, however just about everything for sale can be found there*this includes e-books.

Setting up sales on Fiverr (known as gigs) is relatively straightforward. Just post a picture of your book cover and a simple description of what it's all about. Once a buyer makes their purchase you simply deliver their book copy to them in the form of PDF or DOC file at a profit that is very favorable when compared to Amazon (around four dollars net profit per sale)

*Fiverr works especially well as a source for economical book cover designs too.

12 Ping!

Λ *"ping"* is a XML -based *push mechanism* in which blogs and websites may notify a server (such as google) that new content has been uploaded.

A *ping server* can notify multiple services when pinging such as:

- Search Engines
- Web directories
- News sites
- Aggregators
- Feed sites
- And More

This technology was first introduced in 2001 and today, most blog authoring tools automatically ping one or more servers each time the blogger creates a new post or updates an old one. WordPress most famously does this for you, albeit on a very limited basis. In truth you are better off doing it yourself if you want any real results.*

If you're not the "techie" type, all of this ping talk may be a bit *above your pay grade* and you may be wondering **"what does all this mean to me?"** Suffice it to say that you can use this technology to notify the search engines not only of your latest blog updates or any recent promotional videos or changes to your website, but you can also use it to get your newly uploaded Amazon book's sale page ranked with the search engines faster!

Personally I use **Blast-O-Matic's Commander Edition, one of the best products available for notifying search engines of my newly uploaded books and content. Best of all it's a cell phone-based app that I can use on-the-fly and it works really slick.*

13. Trade reviews with other authors

Hey, we're are all in this together right? I have found that some of the best book reviewers can actually be other book authors. They understand your situation and your need for reviews better than the average reader does. They know that good reviews of the lifeblood of good sales, so it would be to your advantage to reach out and make as many connections with other authors as possible.

Currently Amazon does not allow you to contact other members from within their system so that leaves you searching out other avenues such as Facebook, Twitter and LinkedIn as possible sources. I've even found several budding authors willing to trade review work on YouTube.

Trading reviews should be a *planned event* - often taking a couple weeks to put together - and should not approached haphazardly.

First, gather together a collection of willing authors (10 to 20 should do nicely) and then pick a time scheduled around a five day free giveaway promo event you will set up with your KDP account. At that point you will send your author reviewer list a copy of your free book download link. While you're at it, be sure to find out when their book will be available to return the favor. Then sit back and wait.

Resist the urge to pester or metaphorically "hover" over your reviewer's shoulder. Honest book reviews take time and people have lives to live. Be patient and then if you don't hear back or see any reviews posted after a few weeks, make contact with your missing reviewer and see if you can answer any open questions or at the very least get a fire under their butt!

While there's nothing wrong with an honest review, you should spread this technique around amongst several authors and not build up too much of a "history" with a small group of favorites lest it should appear to Amazon at some point that you're trying to game the system and wind up getting yourself banned from selling as a result!

14. Guest Blog

Submitting articles to other blogs, or better yet, being invited to post articles on other people's blogs is another outstanding way to promote your books and build up your *authority status* at the same time. Alongside of submitting articles to directories (discussed in tip number 17), guest blogging can generate a lot of traffic back to your book's sale page.

Setting yourself up as a guest blogger begins by letting the world know you're available. You can do that I inserting a little blurb right within the pages of your actual book. Something like this works really well:

*"If you'd like to contact me as a source for content for your blog or webpage I'd be happy to speak to you. I can be reached at **GuestBlogger@[your site].com**"*

While you're at it, you can post the same thing on your website, Facebook fan page and yes, even your Amazon author bio!

Don't be too surprised if you get a flood of inquiries hitting your inbox, constantly maintaining new blog content is time consuming work and any smart blog owner will always be on the lookout for a way to lighten his or her load!

15. Always Include Samplers

You should always include at least a chapter or two of any other related books you are offering along with a link to their sale pages in the back of every book you sell*.

This proven technique works so incredibly well that if you do nothing else in this book you will gain additional sales from this one technique alone. The more books you have, the greater the effect will be!

*This has the added benefit of expanding the perceived size of your overall book and page count leading to a justifiably larger price tag too.

16. Set Up Your Author Profile

Take the time to set up your personal bio. This is just another opportunity to highlight yourself as an expert in your field so you should take full advantage of it. Visitors to your book page may feel compelled to know a little bit more about you before making a purchase so this is your chance to put your best foot forward.

When creating your author profile be sure to use a professionally taken picture if possible and make sure that the overall feel of your photo matches the genre of the books you are selling. Obviously a business author's photo will differ greatly from a children's author or romance novelist.

Your profile is where you will also have a chance to list your personal accomplishments as well as any other works available on Amazon.

Currently you can also post promotional YouTube videos as well however this is under review and may not be allowed in the near future due to the abuse.

17. Ezine articles

Article marketing represents an outstanding opportunity to expand your authority status.

By writing a 500 to 600 page article and submitting it to one of the thousands of available article directories found on the web you can create an unlimited number of *back links* to your Amazon sale pages and increase your odds of finding additional buyers.

Every article directory has its own individual rules but most but generally the same. You should strive to be informative and accurate without being too blatantly self-promoting. At the end of the article most directories allow you the space to promote a link. It's here that you will provide a link back to your Amazon books sale page.

Top 20 article directories:

1. ehow.com

2. hubpages.com

3. examiner.com

4. seekingalpha.com

5. ezinearticles.com

6. squidoo.com

7. apsense.com/article/start

8. goarticles.com

9. buzzle.com

10. articlesbase.com

11. technorati.com

12. biggerpockets.com/articles/

13. selfgrowth.com

14. textbroker.com

15. sooperarticles.com

16. brighthub.com

17. knoji.com/articles

19. thefreelibrary.com

20. Infobarrel.com

18. Create A Call To Action

If your book cover design has managed to entice your potential buyer to your sale page you need to be sure to take full advantage of this situation by giving your reader an instruction to *take action* (Ideally, make a purchase) within the books description.

It seems silly to have to *fill in the gaps* for people but you would be surprised how giving the order to BUY NOW can radically effect sales numbers.

I recently did a *split test* using two similar books. Both had essentially the same description and the sales numbers previous to the experiment were pretty much in line with one another. By making one small change, I added the phrase *"**Don't wait – Buy Now**"* to the end of the description of one of the books. No other changes were made.

The results were astounding! Over the next 3 months I witnessed a rise of over 33% more sales in the book featuring the *buy* command.

Powerful stuff…

19. Offer A Test Taste

If you have a sizable work of over 300 pages that is selling a premium price, you could sell a "sampler containing just a few chapters for .99 (or even give it away as often as possible). This will allow potential buyers to experience your work without having to fully commit to a higher price. If readers are impressed with what they see, you're likely to be rewarded with quite a few additional sales. This technique works especially really well with fiction type books.

Word of warning:

You must be sure to **clearly let your buyers know up front that they are *not* purchasing the entire book for .99**. A number of readers probably still won't even see your notice and still expect to get a 300+ page book for $.99 but unfortunately there's little you can do to stop that. The *good news* is even if they leave a bad review it will only be for your sampler and not on your higher-priced work!

20. Design Like A Pro

Your cover is the "face" of your book. When you think about it, This is really about all your sellers have (besides your description) available to them to base a decision on whether or not to purchase your book. People DO judge a book by its cover, so it's to your benefit to make sure that yours is as good as it can possibly be!

A great number of books on Amazon have absolutely lousy covers! It's obvious that the author decided to save a couple of bucks and do it himself using the free tools that came with his computer or worse yet, decided to use Amazon's free cover Creator tool!

If you're going to be serious about selling books you need to be serious about making sure that the entire product is exceptional. Nowhere does this advice apply more than the cover.

If you lack the necessary graphic design capabilities, help is just a click away! Head over to Fiverr.com and check out the multitudes of qualified graphic design artists that can create a professional looking work of art for you starting at just five bucks!

When creating a cover there's a few key tips to remember that will help you maximize sales:

- Make sure the text is readable, even when the graphic is shrunk all the way down to the size of a postage stamp. Amazon displays "thumbnails" in its catalog listings. You want to be sure your book title to stands out - even in its smallest form.

- Skip the urge to use complex graphics. Unless you're doing fictional work there's just no need for it. If you're doing a how-to book or a work of nonfiction, you want your book cover to convey the essence of what your book is about or the problem it solves and nothing more.

- Use contrasting colors. Generally speaking, you should avoid using *half tones* as they tend to blog together, especially when they are shrunk down to a smaller size - at which point they become completely unreadable.

21. Maximize Subtitles

Amazon allows you up to two lines for your books name. You get a *title* line and a *subtitle* line. Your *title line* should be snappy yet it should convey the general idea of what the book is about.

Your *subtitle line* should contain *a longer, more detailed description* and a possible benefit to the reader. Take a look at the example from this book:

33
Things You Can Do
Today To Skyrocket Your
KINDLE SALES

Learn the secrets the pros use to drive sales to incredible levels!

When creating a title for your book you should always *speak to the intended readers need.*

22. Repurpose Old Content

If you currently have an active blog or website that is filled with useful and informative content. You can take a page from many successful Author's playbooks and repurpose that content into one or more e-book collections.*

Repurposed content can be used in many ways:

1. Complete article reprints
2. Collections of topical tips or hints submitted by readers
3. Anthologies
4. "Best of" lists
5. Or just simply quotes

Repurposing old content from your website or blog into a book is also a great way to *brand* your site and draw in new readers. For example, you could create a book called "*The best of xyz.com*" (where XYZ would be the name of your website) this would focus readers attention back to your site as an additional source for on-topic material.

*If you plan on using content that involves submissions from other users you would be wise to post a notice on your website or blog alerting contributors to the fact that upon submission to your site for publication all content becomes your exclusive property. This frees you up to publish without worrying about being sued later on for making a buck off of submitted content.-*Believe me, it can happen!*

23. Partner Up

Joint ventures are hot right now. The only thing more powerful than the effort of one focused person is the effort of *more than one!*

While it's not currently possible to *directly* create joint ventures within the Amazon structure you can still achieve the same outcome by using Amazon affiliate links. In this scenario you would agree with other list owners to promote each other's Amazon offerings via embedded affiliate links to each of your individual buyer lists. Win-win!

An older and more traditional way to do this is to co-author a book together and mutually benefit from the traffic it creates. Inside your book you could make mention of each other's sites or blogs and even go so far as to provide *traceable links* to your readers by using free url shortening services such as **bit.do** or **bit.ly** to measure your co-ventures success.

24. Social Media

No discussion of promotional ideas could truly be complete without at least a brief mention of social media. Readers of my other books are already familiar with my limited use stance concerning Facebook, Twitter, LinkedIn and the rest. I believe they have their place amongst *a well-rounded marketing campaign*, however they should never be used as a one-size-fits-all answer to your promotional needs.

I think too much has been written about how to use social media to promote your business or personal agenda and I find a lot of it to be crap! If you understand what drives the popularity of social media in general its *connections and commonality*. Far too many marketers treat these sites as if they are a deep pool of buyers waiting to be exploited and this is wrong thinking.

Imagine if you will a wine tasting party. The people in attendance all share a common bond (let's say a love of wine for example). The mood is calm and casual and everyone there is generally having a good time discussing their mutual interests. All of a sudden someone kicks open the front door screaming through a bullhorn "***hey everyone, come to my store and buy stuff! It's on sale!***"

Can you imagine the look on the crowd's face? It's highly unlikely anyone would be reaching for their wallets. Yet, this silly example has some clear parallels to the way many people approach marketing to the social media crowd.| It's just plain wrong!

Let's rejoin this party using a different scenario. This time there is no longer anyone *crashing the party*. We were a part of it, moving around, interacting with other attendees, sharing stories and *bonding over commonalities.*

If the opportunity presented itself, perhaps you would take out a business card and casually slip it to another member in attendance as you discuss your shared love of rare French wines as you say *"you know, my store just got one of the only cases still left of Chateau Le Pin- if you're interested in taking a look you should stop by this week."** .... Smooth!

The point I'm making here is to *be a part of the conversation, don't hijack it. Shotgun blasting* your marketing message all over social media is like spinning your tires in the mud, you're doing a lot of work, but you won't get very far.

*Chateau Le Pin: At only 500 to 700 cases a year available worldwide at any given time, you're not getting this stuff at Costco!

25. Broadcast Yourself

Every marketer should have a Youtube channel. You should too! With *zero cost of entry* why wouldn't you want a free opportunity to be listed with the world's second largest search engine?

Besides being able to post an unlimited number of promotional videos, When setting up your channel you also get an opportunity to link potential buyers back to your amazon books sale page or author page (assuming you have more than one book for sale....*and of course you should!*)

If you want to learn how to rapidly crank out several ***mini promotional videos*** for each of your books (and have the added advantage of gaining top search engine ranking in Google as well), check out my book ***How to create a YouTube money machine***, inside I'll teach you my automated template system for producing hundreds of promotional videos a day *plus you get a free two part 30 minute video tutorial as part of the book.*

26. Hold Drawings

People love to win things, so why not use this little bit of knowledge to your promotional advantage?

Bestselling kindle author, Bart Baggett, uses the promise of winning a kindle fire to garner his free book reviews as well as to boost his seller rating at the same time.

His rules require the purchase of a book to be entered into his "drawing". He claims that viewers may post any level of review they like for an equal chance at winning and giveaways are held once a month.

Some may disagree with Bart's methodology and consider it bribery or at least *gaming the review system* but the technique currently complies with Amazons TOS and remains a powerful way to build reviews and pick up sales at the same time.

To learn more about how Bart sets up his system <u>check out his free video here</u>

27. Use Keywords In Your Description

To pull in the maximum number of potential buyers you should always dial in your books description using keywords that are closely related to your niche. The idea keywords are the most often used ones. Finding those keywords is a simple as using Google's *keyword research tool*.

If you don't already have an ad words account head over to adwords.com and get signed up. It's free to use and you don't need to give them any credit card information to take advantage of some truly world class marketing tools.

Once you get signed up find the keyword research tool and enter a few dozen or so key words that are related to your topic to see how they rank. Pick from among the top 10 or so performing keywords and find a way to weave them into your books description. By doing so you will *guarantee* yourself a higher statistic of being found by people searching out those exact keywords, not only in Amazon, but in Google and other search engines as well!

28. Use The Full Description

Speaking of book descriptions, I've seen this time again - book sellers simply throw up a one or two sentence description for their books on the sale page and expect buyers to make a purchase decision based on this minimal information. This is a huge marketing mistake!

If you want to make sales of any respectable size you're going to have to do better than slapping up a short little blurb! You are allowed up to 4000 characters in your description. Don't waste this opportunity. Use every one of them you can. If you can't think of what to say then fall back on the basics. Tell your potential readers:

- **Who** the book is aimed at.

- **What** is the subject matter or better yet, what problems does its content solve.

- **Where** What is the setting for your story or application for your instructional book?

- **When** -This can be interpreted several ways but generally you should convey how up to date the information is (if relevant)

- **Why** readers should listen to you – give your credentials (or you could list your other works here if you are writing nonfiction)

Take a moment and review top Sellers in your category. Check out their descriptions and see how they go about crafting a sales pitch. You don't want to copy their work, but nothing says you can't develop a template for your own book descriptions based upon some commonalities that you find amongst the top performers.

29. Speak!

When I created my book **The30DayBurn,** people wanted to hear more about how I lost over 80 pounds without lifting a finger to exercise. I was invited to speak to all kinds of groups and tell my story. This lead to a natural discussion of my book, and sales followed!

Later, when I began speaking on radio and television interviews, the book link was a little harder to get across. I solved this by linking a domain that pointed directly to the sale page. That way all I had to say was *"You can look me up on Amazon.com or go directly to my sale page at www.The30dayburn.com."**

If you have a book on a teachable subject then take some time to seek out interested groups to tell your story to. You can even offer to speak for free if possible. I like to hand out business cards at my talks that give a direct link to my books on Amazon for those who are interested and want to make a purchase.

*As an author and speaker being able to say your book is available on Amazon lends you tremendous credibility as well!

30. Pitch The Media

The media is a hungry beast. It constantly needs to be fed content in the form of news, entertainment & information. You can help feed that monster by finding ways to tie your various books into current headlines and social movements.

I recall back in 2008 when the economy took another dive, talk of unemployment was everywhere. I used this opportunity to contact the media and send them a press release about my 10 year old son, Chase - who, despite what others were calling a "bad economy" was making an *absolute killing* with his vending business (It's really quite an impressive story. You can check it out here).

The news ran with the story and as expected sales of my book skyrocketed. Back then the book was still only in printed form. These days it's *even easier* to make a sale thanks to Amazon kindle and their genius *one click purchase* set up!

31. Poll Your Readers

Wouldn't it be great if someone would just tell you what topic to write in order to create a best seller? Why not ask your readers? These days it's easier than ever to solicit potential customers for their opinions.

If you are using WordPress to develop your website (Over 70% of the world now is!) you can simply add a freely available ***polling plugin*** to your site that will allow you to *"take the pulse"* of your readers and find out what they are looking for.

Many consumers like to feel their opinion had a hand in shaping a product and because of this many often take a certain "pride *of ownership*" of the finished work. This can have a powerful promotional effect as these dedicated fans will even help you spread the word by tweeting and posting Facebook comments about your book to their own social circles.

32. Keep Updated

Readers like to know that they are purchasing the most recent information on a subject. This advice applies especially to works of a technical or instructional nature.

If there have been recent changes that have taken place since you published your book, you should take the time to go back and update your books content, add chapters, change photos to reflect those most recent changes.

Give your buyers additional assurance they are making a timely decision by letting them know in your books description when your book was last updated.

33. Display Your Updates

Taking tip 32 a bit farther, why not update your cover to reflect any recent changes to the content inside?

Bestselling kindle author Dave Adams does this probably better than anyone I've ever seen. Each time he makes an update to one of his books content he changes a spot he's reserved at the top of the books cover to reflect the date of his most recent change.

Example:
"Last updated July 15th 2015!" This is a really simple idea but you don't see it done too often. If you're selling a book that is in a highly competitive niche, that is constantly changing, then doing something like this could give your buyers a sense of comfort in knowing he or she is getting the freshest, most up to date information available. And that translates to more book sales!

Bonus Idea!

I saved the best for last!

Did you know you can embed YouTube or Vimeo videos within your Amazon book description? Very few authors do. Nothing beats the power of video to make effective sales presentation.

Consider making a mini commercial or trailer about your book and inserting it into the description area for your book. This could create a powerful 1-2 punch for your sales efforts.

Your video could pull *double duty* by being inserted on your mini website you created him tip #3 as well!

Check out this link: **bit.do/skyrocket-1**

Where To Go From Here

I remember years ago when I got into internet marketing. I was overwhelmed by the sheer volume of information that I had to absorb. It seemed insurmountable! I quickly learned to process all these ideas in smaller chunks, implementing them one at a time. Which is why I wrote this book the way I did.

"The journey of a thousand miles begins the first step" as the famous saying goes. There's no right or wrong way to get started but the most important thing you can do is to *actually do it!* Start at the beginning of this book and work your way through each of the ideas. Put each of them to use - one by one and test the results (Progress! - That's the only *true* thing that matters).

As an author you should spend each day taking another step toward building another skill, be it writing or promoting your work. I've been at this since 1992 and when I look back at all that I have learned and accomplished since that time I'm blown away by how much I've learned and managed to do with my daily addition of knowledge!

Now is the time to take that first step.
Here's to your future publishing empire!

If you feel like I've been of help to you I'd like you ask you one small a favor in return;

Please take a moment to leave a positive rating for this book with Amazon so that others will be able to benefit from it as well.

See more recent titles from us

Power Profits!

Power Profits! Cash Flow Revolution

63 Ways to DRIVE MORE TRAFFIC to your website

How to WRITE 30 BOOKS in 30 DAYS

101 TOTALLY FREE ways to market your website or blog

How To Build a YouTube Money Machine

The 10 Principles of ENDLESS WEALTH

For our full catalog visit us at:

2ndEmpireMedia.Com

www.ingramcontent.com/pod-product-compliance
Lightning Source LLC
Chambersburg PA
CBHW070405190526
45169CB00003B/1124